MAKE ME A MILLIONAIRE!

MAKE ME A MILLIONAIRE!

The Treasure Map for future millionaires!

BY

THEODORE PYSH

ISBN-13: 9780692562369
ISBN-10: 0692562362

TABLE OF CONTENTS

PREFACE

So you want to be a millionaire! The sooner the better I suppose. To most of the U.S. middle class, on the surface, $1 million dollars might be considered a fortune. I guess it's all relative. To a person living in poverty $25,000 must seem like a million, though it's barely enough for a new car.

It wasn't too many years ago that National Publishers Clearing House offered a $1 million dollar prize in their sweepstake. The catch was that they paid the money to the lucky winner over 20 years. $1 million dollars paid out over 20 years amounts to $50,000 a year **before** taxes.

After taxes it paid out $31,000 annually. Hardly a millionaire's bounty. Until the Powerball came into play, state lotteries routinely paid out $1 million dollar prizes. The stories are many and varied about lottery winners who went right out and bought cars and houses and were generally broke within 3 years.

This book is about money and building *real* wealth. Or, if you will, a fortune. So first we have to get a proper perspective of just what is *real* wealth.

One hundred years ago, if you had a net worth of $100,000 you were truly wealthy. That same $100,000 adjusted for inflation in 2015 is $2,324,871.28. A nice sum of money but it would hardly categorize you as wealthy (a loaf of bread in 1915 cost 7 cents).

Consider this: If you're a 35 year old male and you have $2 million dollars in tax free cash, could you retire and live on the beach? Maybe, but you wouldn't be living the high life.

The average life expectancy of today's male is 77 years. That gives you 42 years to live on your stash. If you took the money in 42 equal annual installments to age 77, you'd be enjoying $47,619.05 per year (a loaf of bread today is about $3.50). And heaven help you if you live to 78!

So, no retirement for you with a paltry $2 million in the bank. There are many wonderful things in this life that have nothing to with money. To find those things, you will have to purchase a different book. While there are miserable millionaires and happy Zen Buddhists; this book is about money and wealth and little else. We'll help you find the money, you'll have to find the happiness.

So, let's start making you a millionaire!

Chapter 1

INSTANT GRATIFICATION
"LIFE'S RECIPE FOR FAILURE"

From our earliest years on this planet most of us are weaned on instant gratification. You cry as a baby and mom feeds you, or at least puts a pacifier in your mouth. As we grow, many of us learn that if we cry or pout enough, our parents will provide the balm we're looking for to take away our pain, real or imagined.

This isn't good training for the future. That's not to say we should just leave a baby crying but at some point we need to be taught that instant gratification is almost never the best way to live life. It certainly will be a barrier to entry in the fortune club.

Saving up your pennies for the things you really want rather than your parents just buying them for you on your whim has a real sense of satisfaction and joy not available to you if you get what you want when you want it.

If you really, truly want to accumulate millions, you will need to discipline yourself to reject and recognize when you are taking the "short term payoff" rather than the more satisfying and sensible long term reward.

Because the "short term payoff" comes in many disguise and immediately excites the dopamine in our brain, it is sometimes difficult to recognize or even pay attention to the fact that we are "opting out" of the better alternative.

Some examples:

* Gas cost $3.15 a gallon all over town. But you find an outlet that charges just $3.00! Good for you. You fill your tank and pay for it with a credit card because you don't want to use your cash on hand right now. The credit card charges 15% interest and you don't pay the balance off in full each month. That gas just cost you $3.45 a gallon! $ .30 cents more than the highest price in town. *Short term pay off, long term pain*

* Would you intentionally throw away a million bucks? You graduate from High School and

go right into the work force. You're tired of studying. You've secured a job that pays "good money" *but not as good as it would be.*

In a lifetime, (working 40 years) a High School graduate, on average, will make $1.2 million dollars. A college graduate with just a Bachelor's degree will make $2.1 million. You don't think you're average? Neither did the millions of others in this study. Even an associates degree or two year technical school will get you at least $325,000 or even more over your working life time. You just threw away $1 million dollars and didn't even know it. And if you did know it, shame on you*! Short term pay off, long term pain.*

(That's not to say that you must have a good education to accumulate millions of dollars. Many have done it without even a high school education. But you make it exponentially harder for yourself to get there; simply because an education imparts knowledge to you that you'll have to learn on your own over a longer period of time. The degree provides you with a larger base capital to start on your road to Fortune.)

* A young lady wins $5,000 on a lottery scratch ticket. She knows she'll have to pay taxes on

the winnings but that's not till the end of the year. So she spends all the money on a vacation, some new clothes and a big screen TV. But time flies! Before you know it the tax man wants his $2000 cut. She doesn't have it. He doesn't have a sense of humor. So she takes a cash advance on a credit card at 20% interest to pay the tax. *Short term payoff, long term pain.*

And it isn't just a money thing!

* Two young people get caught up in the passion of the moment and despite knowing the possible consequences, they have unprotected sex. The girl becomes pregnant. Or the boy acquires an STD or worse. *Short term payoff, long term pain.*
* An individual is at a party one night. There's plenty of liquor and he drinks himself silly because it feels good. On the way home the police pull him over.

    There's a breath test. He's over the limit. DUI. Big Fine! Possible jail time! His insurance rates go to the moon! That was some expensive liquor. *Short term pay off, long term pain.*

* The teenager buys a cheap stereo system for his car because he wants it now. He just can't wait until he has enough money for the premium system. He installs it and the sound is distorted and unpleasant. "Buy nice or buy twice!" *Short term pay off, long term pain.*

There is a difference between intelligence and wisdom. If I were made to choose between the two I would choose wisdom. And fortunately wisdom can be acquired, while intelligence cannot. Some are blessed with both but the world is full of smart people who make unwise choices.

The wise individual is constantly weighing the long term consequences of one action (or inaction) over another.

True Story: I personally know an individual who sold his business in 2001 for $30 million. He then proceeded to build a 15,000 square foot mansion; partial ownership in a jet plane, expensive cars and *real* expensive jewelry for his wife, a condo for his father, and a home for his in laws. He didn't pay cash for his father's condo but rather mortgaged it. Same thing for his in laws. By 2004 he had literally spent it all. They evicted his 92 year old father out of his Florida condo and foreclosed on the house he mortgaged for his in laws. In the end, he went to federal prison for tax evasion.

Now, this man was smart. He grew a business from nothing in just 3 years and found a buyer who would pay millions. But I think we can all agree he was **unwise**. *Short term payoff...Well, you know.*

Perhaps now he's acquired wisdom. Let's hope.

If you notice that your life is, for the most part, built around instant gratification, you must change this lifestyle or you have no chance of ever acquiring wealth except through an enormous amount of luck. And even in that situation you're not likely to keep your wealth. i.e. the lottery winner.

Even something as seemingly trivial as a cigarette habit can seep into your future and keep you from your opportunities to achieve real wealth.

Consider this: Why does one smoke cigarettes? Because of the *short term* pleasure it gives him or her. Research has found that the poorer you are, the more likely you are to smoke. We also know that the average smoker goes through about a pack and a half a day.

Today, a pack of cigarettes costs about $5.00. That's $7.50 a day for the average smoker.

It's costing that individual $2,730 annually in money that is literally going up in smoke. Let's remind you that the person who's spending that money is usually the one who can least afford it.

We aren't even going into the dollars they must spend on health care to treat the many chronic, even life threatening conditions caused by tobacco use. *Short term pay off, long term pain.*

(I'm not saying if that person doesn't quit smoking that they can't be rich. Though they will be $2,730 richer; and if you found $2730 lying on the street today, you'd probably think you were having a pretty good afternoon. But a person stuck at the bottom of the economic ladder generally will opt for the short term pleasure to ease the pain of

poverty that's constantly sitting on their shoulder. If this is you, and you truly want to be wealthy, you must make yourself reject as much of this behavior as you're able. There is a difference between **want** *and* **need**.)

> *"Heaven help me for the way I am.*
> *Save me from these evil deeds before I get them done.*
> *I know tomorrow brings the consequence at hand.*
> *But I keep living this day like the next will never come."*
> *(Fiona Apple, "Criminal")*

All of this is not to say that one should *never* opt for the short term pay out. Sometimes it's appropriate and even wise. But when you have two options, and the short and long term outcomes could be markedly different, both should be considered before choosing. A consistent lifestyle of short term payouts and instant gratification is life's recipe for failure.

So, before we begin your journey to the Fortune Club, it's good to know what's going to stand in your way. Only you and bad choices can hold you back.

"Time is Money" Spend it well!

Chapter 2

THE FIRST RULE OF MONEY
"MONEY GOES TO THE PROXIMATE"

Any seasoned banker knows this is the first rule of money. But what do we mean by "Money goes to the Proximate?" it's simple really, *it means the closer you are to the money the more likely you are to get it.*

Let's say the young man who lives down the block from you has a widowed mother worth millions of dollars. When she passes (or decides to start distributing the money), who is more likely to be the beneficiary? You or her only son? After all, you just live a block away.

Obviously, you're not getting any of it. Charity might get some but unless she and her son are estranged (and maybe not even then) he's going to get it all. *"Money goes to the proximate"*

Maybe you're married to a wealthy individual. The marriage falls apart. What do you get? Half! *"Money goes to the proximate"*

Advice I gave my daughter: *"Never marry for money; hang around rich people, then marry for love."* (No, she didn't listen but she *is* happily married)

The man or woman who is born into or marries into wealth has a distinct economic advantage over the rest of us. They are close to the money.

But maybe more important than the proximity to the *money* are the *opportunities* provided to extend and create wealth not available to the lower classes.

To demonstrate the significant advantage of being born into wealth, let's look at some real life examples of these distinct advantages and opportunities that come with being well born:

At the time of this writing, the richest man on the planet earth is a fellow named Bill Gates.

Mr. Gates' net worth is estimated to be about $80 billion dollars. He is arguably a genius, scoring 1590 out of 1600 on his college SAT scores. In addition he has, and has always had, incredible business acumen. But William Gates III has never been wanting for wealth and, beyond his obvious intelligence and street smarts he inherited a big boost to his future fortunes.

Mr. Gates' real break in business came in 1980 when he was able to sign a licensing agreement with IBM to provide an operating system for their new IBM PC.

Let's compare Bill Gates and a typical, middle class individual with comparable intelligence and similar business sense both living in Seattle in 1981.

Andy Average lives a comfortable, middle class life. He's 24 years old (the same age as Bill Gates was at the time he signed with IBM.) He enjoys an IQ of 155 and has run his own software company since he was 19.

This is where the similarities end.

Bill Gates' father is a prominent Seattle lawyer and his mother serves on the board of directors of First Interstate BancSystem and the United Way. Gates' maternal grandfather was a national bank president.

Andy Averages' father is a mail carrier and his mom is a nurse at a local Seattle hospital.

Both Andy and Bill become aware that IBM is looking for an operating system for their new Personal Computer (PC) product.

Andy and Bill both believe they have the solution to the IBM dilemma. 24 year old Andy, makes multiple phone calls to IBM headquarters in Armonk, New York but fails in his attempt to reach someone who can facilitate his presentation to the person or persons who are in charge of this project. However, in her rolodex, Bill's mother has access to senior level executives at IBM.

The rest, as they say, is history.

The Andy Average story is, of course, fictional. However, the fact that Mr. Gates' mother intervened in the communication with IBM executives is rumored to be true. It certainly seems plausible. How else does an unknown 24 year old in Seattle get in front of the IBM project managers?

When it was all said and done, Bill Gates purchased all rights to the base programming software for MS DOS (Microsoft Disc Operating System) from a company called Seattle Computer Products for $50,000 and that software was what was used to operate the first IBM PCs. That would be $136,000 in today's dollars. Where did 24 year old Bill Gates obtain today's equivalent of $136,000 cash to make this purchase in 1981?

This is not to say that William Gates III isn't an economic titan. He was, and of course, still is. His wealth has far surpassed that of his parents due largely to his own efforts. But one wonders if he could have accomplished this if his mom were a nurse and father a mail carrier.

"Money (and opportunity) goes to the proximate"

How about Warren Buffett? Arguably the greatest investor of all time. There is absolutely no debate over Mr. Buffett's business acumen. He's the reigning king of Wall Street.

But when did he get started? His company, Berkshire Hathaway, was founded in 1955. In 1957 he started his first big partnership. He asked a physician friend to get 10 other doctors to invest $10,000. ($85,000 in 2015 dollars). Warren himself had only invested $100 of his own money. The 26 year old Warren Buffett got 11 doctors to invest and away they went to riches!

But how was a 26 year old able to connect with wealthy doctors and persuade them to invest $10,000 with him?

Maybe it was because Mr. Buffett's father was a United States Congressman who "may" have called in a few chips and asked his wealthy colleagues to talk with his son.

How many wealthy individual numbers does your mail carrier father have in his contact list?

This is in no way meant to disparage the genius or accomplishments of Mr. Buffet,

It's just one more "true life" example of how *"Money goes to the proximate."*

We assume that if you're reading this book, you were not born with a silver spoon in your mouth. So, are you financially doomed? Of course not! You don't *have* to be close to the money to acquire a fortune any more than you need a chain saw to cut a log. But it does make things a lot easier. Anyway, just because you weren't *born* close to the money, doesn't mean you can't *be* close to the money.

I'm not talking about being devious or making fake friendships with wealthy individuals, though the "tongue in cheek" advice I gave my daughter italicized earlier in this chapter wasn't as exaggerated as one might think. You have to find the money and then get close to it.

Hmm…we might need a treasure map.

Ok, how about this: If you're a young adult, don't apply to flip burgers at McDonalds (rich people don't go there often) Instead, apply to wait tables at the nearest Country Club! Get the point?

Maybe you'll wait on some rich guy who takes a liking to the way you fold napkins and he decides to take you under his wing. (You're getting *closer*!) Or maybe you'll serve some handsome rich boy who likes your smile.

Meanwhile, almost 20% of billionaires have made their money in **Finance**. Does that mean banking? Well, not exactly. We're talking brokerage firms and Hedge Funds.

You may not even know what a Hedge fund is, and that's not important. What's important is that you find a job at one of these doing whatever menial work they assign you.

Know this: *The children of wealth will be working right beside you or a notch up on the ladder because their parents may have some influence and that's where the big money is.*

At a brokerage firm or investment bank like Goldman Sachs or JP Morgan, you are very close to untold millions.

A 22 year old first year rookie, straight out of college, who lands a job at a Wall Street brokerage firm will be assigned a cubicle from which to work and a $600,000 base salary. And he's low man on the totem pole!

Assuming you don't live and aren't planning to move to New York City, there are many other areas and places you can go.

Speaking of which, the *real* value of a Harvard education isn't so much the curriculum, though that's top drawer, it's more the networking you get to do. When you go to an Ivy League school your class-mates are going to be the sons and daughters of high ranking executives in all sorts of fields.

They graduate, they go to work for their father's company; and tell their dad all about their friend Bob or Roberta with whom they went to school and how you would fit just perfect in that new opening.

But the shortest *legal* way to making a fortune is to start your own business. Most of the wealthy individuals in this country are business owners. Remember, that's what Bill Gates and Warren Buffet did. When you do, you should belong to as many civic clubs as possible and attend as many events as you're able. The Chamber of Commerce, Kiwanis, Elks, City Council meetings, Mayoral events, whatever. Somewhere in those organizations is a hidden gem of a person with a lot of money who just happens to like the way you smile.

What do you need them for? To make your small business bigger. To connect you to people who can provide you more and bigger revenue.

Believe this: They're there. Particularly the city fathers who pull most of the triggers to wealth in the community. They're giving back through community involvement and contribution.

That's not to say you should be a predator and just attack the first guy you see who looks like money but a casual dialogue will eventually turn up someone who will facilitate your road to fortune. *"Money goes to the proximate."*

So, we know it facilitates things when you're closer to the money but that doesn't mean you can't still find your fortune without an education or marrying into wealth.

Here are some encouraging facts:

* There are 12 million millionaires on the planet. (Surely you can find ONE who likes you!)
* There are 2,325 billionaires
* 35% of billionaires don't hold a college degree
* The University of Pennsylvania has the most billionaire alumni, followed by Harvard and Yale.
* America has more billionaires than any other country. As of this writing there are 571 billionaires in the U.S.
* 60% of billionaires made their wealth themselves.
* The average billionaire is 63 years old.
* 93% of billionaires are over 45
* 63% are married
* Billionaires tend to purchase real estate

Guys and Gals who made it on their own:

* **Jan Koum**, the CEO and cofounder of "WhatsApp" once lived on food stamps before Facebook made him a billionaire.
  Net worth: $7.7 billion
* **Jack Ma** taught English before founding Alibaba in 1999. Ma grew up in poverty. He failed the national college entrance exams twice!
  Net worth: $20.2 billion

* **Elizabeth Holmes** started her blood diagnostics company when she was 19. Now at 30, she's a billionaire.

  Net worth: $4.5 billion

* **Starbucks' Howard Schultz** grew up in a housing project for the poor. Shortly after college graduation he took over a coffee shop called Starbucks, which at the time had 60 units. He became CEO in 1987 and Starbucks now has more than 16,000 outlets worldwide.

  Net worth: 2.1 billion

  Notice that all of these individuals started their own enterprise. Throw in a Warren Buffett and Bill Gates and you can see that starting your own operation, be it a software company or a coffee shop is your very best and shortest road to real wealth.

  But it's not the *only* way. You can still accumulate a fortune working for a large corporation through proper planning and discipline. It's just going to take longer.

There are plenty of *illegal* ways to make money really fast. But beware, if you get caught, (And sooner or later you will) your chance at a fortune just dropped like a rock in the ocean. Besides, it's seldom what it seems: *The average drug dealer clears about $20,000 a year.*

There are several professions that will take you off course to riches:

Want to be a

* **News correspondent?** $35,600 Annual Income
* **Radio Announcer?** $29,020
* **State Legislator?** $20,620
* **Emergency Medical Technicians?** $31,500
* **Pre-School Teacher?** $27,570
* **Architect?** $79,300

These are all "mean" salaries. Half make more, half less. From the above, the architect makes the most. However, this individual must go to school for 8 years before he or she makes that "mean" $79k. Starting salary is about $44,000. **"Time is money" Spend it well.**

Chapter 3

"LIVING IN THE PETTY CASH DRAWER OF LIFE!"

I presume if you chose to read this book, you haven't yet made your fortune. Do you wonder what's been holding you back? Youth? Age? Parents? Spouse? Kids? Education?

"The search for blame is always successful." (Robert Half)

To begin, on the socioeconomic (big word huh?) ladder the lower you start, the bigger the odds are against you ever being wealthy. In fact, only a very small percentage will make it higher than two rungs up. Researchers at Stanford University have found that children raised in low-income families will most likely have low incomes as adults. This research also showed that the expected income for individuals raised in well-off families is about 200% larger than the expected income of children raised in poor families and about 75% larger than that of persons raised in middle-class families.

So if you were born into a poor family, you have your work (pun intended) cut out for you.

Alright! Here's the socioeconomic (there's that word again) ladder:

UPPER CLASS
MIDDLE UPPER CLASS
LOWER UPPER CLASS
UPPER MIDDLE CLASS   > (This is as far as you go)
MIDDLE MIDDLE CLASS
LOWER MIDDLE CLASS > (Born here?)
UPPER LOWER CLASS
MIDDLE LOWER CLASS
LOWER CLASS

There're those two rungs up the ladder we talked about on the last page.

Even to get up two rungs to Upper Middle Class from where you start will take a serious effort. Donald Trump was born into MIDDLE UPPER CLASS so the jump to riches was just a skip up one rung! Same for Bill Gates and Warren Buffett but probably not you. So, you're not likely to acquire millions from where you started

Unless:

You have a treasure map!

And it just so happens there's one in your hand.

First we have to get you out of the petty cash drawer of life. Many years ago, a fellow named Napoleon Hill wrote a book called "Think and grow Rich." The concept was simple enough. Just think big and big things will come to you. But you may have a real mental block about thinking big. As a child, you may have had an unspoken "script" engraved in your brain by an adult that won't let you think big. If you were born into the lower classes the script may have gone like this: *"Work real hard but don't you dare try to get rich! You can live a comfortable life but rich is for the Kennedy's, not for people like us."* There's an old saying, *"Own the child, own the man!"*

My father was a coal miner. (upper lower class) $100 seemed like a mountain of money to me well into my young adult life. Later, I was a self-made millionaire; b ut it took me almost 56 years! I went from

UPPER LOWER CLASS coal miner's son all the way up to LOWER UPPER CLASS business executive and I learned a lot about how to get there. Today, I'm working on the next million. But I had a hell of a time getting over in my mind that I wasn't allowed to get rich 'cause that's for the Kennedys and Gates and Buffetts.

Anyway, if you don't have millions yet then you probably don't have the road map. That's why you paid me for this book, so I have a responsibility to deliver the millionaire GPS. Think I'm too old and out of touch?

Let me remind you:

Even Tiger woods pays for golf lessons! Serena Williams has a tennis coach. So do Lebron James and Jim Brady. The coaches don't play as well but they know how to make them better. Anyway, I know you don't have 56 years to get there so let this handbook be your short cut.

So enough of this! We have to hurry! Time to get you out of the petty cash drawer so we can get you *your* first million as soon as possible. By the way, we don't mean next Wednesday. It's still gonna take a little while.

Now let me introduce you to the concept of:

"Anchoring"

"Anchoring" is a marketing term that we can apply to your financial mind set.

Human beings generally *anchor* on a number. Here's an example: You walk into a store and purchase a blender for $29.95, one nickel away from $30 bucks.

But depending on where you live, with sales tax, that blender actually cost you more like $32 and change.

Anyway, you bring it home and your roommate says: *"Nice blender! What'd it cost?"* You say: *"Twenty Nine Bucks!"* What? Did you forget about the other 3 bucks? (Yes! You did) What you've done, and what any marketing expert will tell you you've done, is *anchor* on the first numbers. You didn't even think about the $.95 part! Why doesn't the price tag just say $30? Because it's easier for you to purchase the blender at $29.95!

The way it's presented can be deceptive. For instance, the word *hundred* sounds like lot less than the word *thousand* even when the price is higher.

If a sales clerk tells you a big screen TV *"costs one thousand dollars,"* doesn't it sound like more than *twelve hundred fifty?* But twelve hundred fifty is 25%

more than a thousand! The difference is the word *hundred*, even lots of hundreds sounds like less than the word "*thousand.*" Which sounds better? "*The price is one thousand four hundred ninety five dollars*" or "*The price is fourteen hundred ninety five dollars?*" We could even take both words out and say "*The price is fourteen fifty!*" And while we're at it, $1450 sounds like less than $1400!

The consumer *anchors* on the 17 and psychologically throws away the 50. So, if it's "yes, I'll buy it" at $1700 it's also "yes" at $1750, so you might as well get the extra $50!

So, let's see how or if it applies to you. Unless you're super rich or too young to be super rich then you have an anchor.

You have a sticker price that you made yourself and pasted on your emotional chest. And the first number is your anchor.

What's your current income? That's your price tag. That's your *Anchor.* If you make $30,000 a year that's exactly what you think you're worth and you're anchored on $30 something.

"*But!*" you say, "*I think I'm worth more than that but that's all this stupid company will pay me!*" Ok. How much? $35k? it can't be much more than that. And if you got a $5 thousand dollar raise, you'd probably be thrilled and stay on the job a lot longer. That, my friend, is the financial kiss of death. *I thought you wanted to make a million!* You have to raise your anchor above the 30 mark or 40 mark or whatever it is today.

You may have to start your own business on the side until you can grow it to a full time enterprise and quit this job. You may have to acquire a new skill set so what you do is worth more. "You can't be sticking around with a $30 or $40,000 anchor, that's pocket change!

Know what your home is worth? It's worth exactly what someone will pay for it and not a penny more!

Know what your skills are worth? The same! So you can't let the market dictate your income!

Meanwhile, there is so much money out there for those who go for it. And those who *believe* they deserve it. You deserve it and you have to recognize that fifty or a hundred thousand dollars is chump change. At this point this handbook would like to show you just how much is available for you.

Right now, there's about $60 trillion dollars circulating around the globe!

In the U.S. alone there is $1.2 trillion which includes the coins and bills in people's pockets and money under mattresses. Just to give you a proper perspective, it would take you 31,000 years to count to a trillion.

If you made $429,000 a month, would you be happy? To date, Donald Trump has never filed *personal* bankruptcy. But, since 1991, he has filed *business* bankruptcy 4 times.

As the story goes, the first time he negotiated with the bankers who financed his now defunct Taj Mahal Casino, they decided to restrict Mr. Trump's lifestyle. They allowed him only $429,000 a month for living expenses and not a penny more until he got things right again. And this was more than 25 years ago! (In 2015 dollars that's $752,872.55 a month) $429,000 a month is punishment? I want *that* banker. But seriously, it really goes to show that up there in the financial sky there's some real heavy buckets of money just thrown away.

The point is this: With $60 trillion dollars floating around don't you think you should get your head right and grab a few million of it? Why not you? If you don't, someone else will be happy to take *your* share!

And just what *is* your share? It's whatever you truly believe it is. Believe enough to go after it and not be afraid of it. At the upper class level of the world we live in, a hundred million dollars is a hiccup. *"But I'm not at the upper level!"* you say. Well, you have the handbook! Did you think this would be easy? Start moving!

Billionaire Jan Koum did! And he was living on food stamps!

Billionaire Jack Ma did! And they turned him down for a job at Kentucky Fried Chicken!

Billionaire Howard Schultz did! And he grew up in the projects!

They didn't get rich quick, and it's not likely you will either but none of these guys are old men.

You have to work smart. Working hard is a virtue of sorts and usually necessary but "smart work trumps hard work!"

The janitor in the office building makes $25,000 a year. The stockbroker down the hall makes $250,000 a year. Does the stockbroker work 10 times harder than the janitor? In the coming chapters, I will show you more specifically how to acquire your fortune and how to recognize and avoid the traps that would set you back. It's time to stop living in *the petty cash drawer of life.*

Chapter 4

"MAKING MONEY
WHILE YOU SLEEP"

Contrary to what some believe, everyone on this planet gets 24 hours a day. Nobody gets a bonus 25 and nobody gets cheated down to 23. You'll be happy to know that we've allocated 24 hours for you too.

But we have a financial problem here. Thousands of wise money managers have said this tens of thousands of times 'cause it's true: *"Time is Money"*

In that 24 hours you are going to have to sleep at least 6 hours a day to get by. (The experts prefer we get 8 but ok, we'll settle for 6.) We all know people who claim to get by on 3 or 4 hours sleep but that's just a damn lie! In fact, sleep deprivation is a form of torture.

So let's allocate your share of sleep to just 6 hours. If it's true that *"Time is money"* then even with the *"We don't recommend it"* 6 hours, we're wasting 25% of our productive, money making moments!

I know there are rare exceptions like some world renowned brain surgeon but those dudes aside; it's darn near impossible to get *real* wealth just doing your day job.

Oh, you can be financially *comfortable* but is that really what you want? Then why'd you buy this book? You know what financially *comfortable* is? It's settling for financial mediocrity. It's the best of the worst and the worst of the best!

Let's say you have an executive position and it pays you really well; $100,000 a year! Well, that does put you in the top 5% of income in the U.S. But, if you just settle for that and your annual 2% raise you have absolutely no chance of getting into the wealth club.

You have to take advantage of that wasted 25% time and without losing sleep, make money while your head's on the pillow. You don't have to quit your executive job (or any job) but you have to find some way to use those 6 or 8 hours and make money while you're sleeping. *"Well, how do I do that?"*

I'll show you.
Your employer pays you a set amount for a set amount of time for a day's work. He or she will probably not hand over a million dollar bonus anytime soon.

(If she does, please keep your job, disregard anything you've read so far and pass this book on to someone who needs it.)

For the few of us who aren't lucky enough to have that certain employer it goes like this: *When you stop working your employer stops paying.*

You have to find something that will pay you when you stop being personally productive. When you and your skill set need a rest. The good news is, if you sit down and think about it, you'll figure out that something you have or can acquire that will pay you while you cruise around the world. (It's just a figure of speech, you can't do that anyway...yet)

I'm going to show you lots of examples but here's the first one: *This book!* Right now, there are 7.3 billion people on this earth. Tens of millions of those are buying books today. I only need a very small fraction of those millions to buy it and I'm in tall cotton! (In the South that's slang for "getting rich!")

Someone in another time zone could be purchasing this book while I slumber! Or, I might be playing golf! After all, I don't have to go to work. I wrote my book. I paid my dues and the world is gonna pay me whether I sleep or golf or fish or just meet a friend for a long lunch.

But what if my book isn't a best seller? Well, my Pay Pal account is still growing like a taxi meter even though it may not be making millions. And I "do" have other income. What if you had this book *and* your job? Say it provided a modest couple of thousand dollars a month. You wouldn't be financially independent but you'd be well on your way! Write some more!

Ok, so you can't write a book. Well, I can't write computer code either. And you don't want to ride in any rocket ships I build. I know you have other marketable skill sets and ideas. Maybe some you never thought about or even knew you had. That's what "Shark Tank" is all about. Maybe you can make a hit CD and sit back and collect royalties!

Can't sing? Darn! Well ok. But It wouldn't take much money to invest in a couple and then a couple more vending machines you can put in an office building.

They'll be buying your potato chips and candy bars while you're on the golf course! (Getting in reach now, isn't it?)

Another true story: Not long ago some 23 year old kid in Vietnam made a video game called "Flappy Bird." At its peak, it generated $250,000 a day while he slept! (Or partied, who knows?)

Coming up with a 24/7 money making idea is probably the best and fastest way to acquire your fortune. Maybe license your new software. (That's what Bill Gates did!) But if you don't have an idea or a great recording voice, or know how to market yourself; not to worry, because it's not the *only* way.

Warren Buffett made his billions through investing. He's in his 80's now but he was a millionaire by age 31. Not bad. But he didn't start investing with millions. In fact, his first investment was at age 11. He bought 3 shares of Cities Service Preferred for himself and 3 shares for his sister Doris. When he was 14 years old he bought a 40 acre farm with $1200 of his savings. By the time he finished college, Buffett had accumulated more than $100,000 in savings measured in 2015 dollars.

He made money while he was sleeping. His stock and his real estate both went up in value while he slept. He sold them all for a handsome profit. (though we're told that to this day he regrets selling his Cities Service stock)

Mr. Buffett started with $1200 bucks.

By investing wisely you can make millions before you're too old to enjoy it. And you can snore away while it happens.

In the coming chapters I'm going to show you all the different ways and things (called asset classes) you can invest in to get you to Millionaire Land. I'm also going to show you which investments (and individuals) will cause you to lose sleep. Those you will need to avoid.

Remember, right now, as you read this there's some $60 trillion dollars just floating around in liquid form all around you! It's looking for places to go. Why not say: *"Hey! Look over here!"* You can't have it all but you can have all you need or want If you make wise decisions.

Perhaps best of all, you'll still leave trillions for others.

Chapter 5

"UNWISE DECISIONS"
(THINGS AND PEOPLE TO AVOID)

I n a long journey, to get from point "A" to point "B" it's helpful to have a map that will show you where there are detours, toll roads and places to avoid. I hope you will consider this chapter to be your "Map to Millions," pointing out the "Barriers to Entry" into the millionaires club.

"Big Hat, No Cattle"
The men and women of the cattle industry have a saying for the dudes who talk a big game about their holdings but basically have really nothing to show for

it. "Big hat, no cattle." You can pretty much guess what that means.

You know the people who *talk* about how much money they have? They're broke. Not "maybe," not "It seems like it" not "Gee I wonder?" They're broke. Count on it!

Same goes for the ones who say "Money's no problem," It's no problem 'cause they don't have any. The rare possible exception to this is Donald Trump and even he's filed business bankruptcy 4 times and stuck his creditors with millions of unpaid bills.

Run away from any financial dealings with anyone who speaks in this tongue. They will hurt you. They will use you. They will hurt you financially, emotionally and rob you of your spirit.

People with real wealth are usually very secretive about it. They "cry poor" and many actually believe they're near poor even though they're worth millions.

In 1924, Sebastian S. Kresge, the founder of K-Mart stores, was worth $375 million dollars ($5.6 billion in 2015 money). Yet he would not play golf as he thought the cost of replacing lost golf balls was too dear.

Nelson Bunker Hunt was an American Oil company executive worth billions. In the 1970s He and his brother, tried to corner the global silver market. In the last 9 months of 1979 they had made an estimated $4 billion in profit in the silver market accumulating approximately 100 million troy ounces of silver.

Primarily because of their accumulation of the precious metal, the price of silver bullion went from $11 an ounce in September of 1979 to $50 an ounce (the highest price ever recorded for silver) by January 1980!

Two months later, the price of silver collapsed to below $11 an ounce in one day. It was the largest single one day drop in history and it was labeled "Silver Thursday"

Mr. Hunt filed for bankruptcy protection in 1988 mostly due to lawsuits as a result of his silver speculation.

Anyway, don't cry for Mr. Hunt. At that level of wealth bankruptcy works differently than it does for common folk. He and his brother Wilber still had plenty of cash and assets.

On May 2nd 1980, he and his brother Herbert were hauled up in front of a House Sub Committee and they asked Nelson and Wilber some really pointed financial questions about their assets.

The following isn't an exact transcript of the questioning but it captures the flavor of how things went. However, Mr. Hunt's last answer in this interrogatory is a true quote.

* **Mr. Hunt you own some oil fields in Texas. Can you tell me what they're worth?**
* *"Hmm...I would say between $40 and $50 million."*
* **All right! I also see you own hundreds of Thoroughbred horses. Any idea of their worth?**
* *"Probably somewhere around the $40 million dollar range"*
* **You also have an 8,000 acre blue grass farm in Lexington Kentucky. Can you share with us how much it's worth?**
* *"Hmm...maybe $15million???"*
* **Mr. Hunt! Do you mean to tell me you don't know what your properties are worth?**

(To this, Mr. Hunt gave the infamous answer)

* *"Sir, I think you'll find that a man who knows exactly what he's worth isn't worth very much!"*

* Beware the individual who brags they have money. Those who have it seldom speak of it and usually aren't ostentatious. (Whew! What's that mean?) Once, I stood next to Warren Buffett in a jewelry store. He was wearing an inexpensive, untucked, yellow polo shirt with a stain.

Anyway, stay away from those big money talkers and remember this:

"Money Screams! Wealth is Silent."

This brings us to:

Credit Cards
(The legal thieves)

It's been written that the average American has 8 credit cards in their wallet. I'm sure I don't have to elaborate on what a bad idea that is.

Today, almost everyone needs a credit card of some sort. Visa, Mastercard, American Express or whatever.

Know this, the bank that issues your credit card is not your friend, not your partner, not your anything except your creditor. They don't care about you.

And no matter how funny their commercials may be ("What's in your wallet?") there's nothing funny about how they do business.

Be just one day late with a payment and you'll get dinged with a $35 charge. (If that happens to you, be sure to call them, they'll usually waive the fee if it hasn't happened before.)

They'll tease you with 0% interest rates for one year. Then, many will hit you with 29% interest if you don't pay the bill in the first year.

I know you think you will, but you won't, and they know you won't too.

However, you need to have *some* kind of credit card so you can have some kind of credit score. 90% of credit decisions are made off what is called your FICO score.

In addition, there are some purchases, especially airfare, hotels, rent a cars and the like that truly *require* a credit card to make a purchase. Walk up to a rental car counter and hand them $1000 cash and they *still* won't rent you a car.

Hand them a credit card with a $300 limit and they'll happily send you on your way in a brand new whatever car you like.

Think of this: Right now, most banks pay 0% interest on the money they borrow from the Fed. (And by the way, banks have credit ratings too!) If they charge you just 14% on your credit card, they're making a 1,400% profit if you don't pay that card off at the end of the month.

There are darn few businesses (in fact I can't think of one) besides banks that can make that kind of profit. There's a line on financial statements that says COGS or "Cost Of Goods Sold"

The banks "product" is money. They sell money. What is the cost of goods they borrow to sell to you? If it's not money they lend you from a depositor, the cost is Nothing.

At the time of this writing, the Federal Reserve lets banks borrow money at 0%. So they lend it to you on your credit card at 14% or even higher! (I know some as high as 29.9%).

You're not gonna get your millions this way. We need to go back to the first chapter to see what happens here.

You buy a blouse at a department store for $30 because it's on sale 20% off. You put it on your credit card. Your credit card charges 20% on unpaid balances. Unless you pay your credit card balance in full at the end of the month, (and it's unlikely) You just paid the same as if the blouse was never on sale.

How about this: You owe $3000 on a credit card @ 20% interest. You make the required minimum payment of $75. Of that payment, $50 goes to interest. Your $75 has paid down the balance to $2975. At that rate, it will take you something like 30 years and thousands of dollars in interest just to pay off $3000.

Believe this: You can't make money in the stock market or anywhere else that will beat what you're paying on that credit card interest. Even if it's just 14 or 15%! The answer here is to pay your credit card balance in full as soon as you can and preferably by the end of the month.

Some individuals take their credit card(s) and put them in the freezer until they need them. This pretty much eliminates "impulse" buying because they have to take the card(s) out of the freezer and let them thaw until they can be used.

The New Car
My old college professor used to say "Never use absolutes!" Get it? "Never" *is* an absolute. But I'm going

to violate that rule just like he did. NEVER buy a new car! One of the worst ways to spend money is on a new car. Know why? First, when you drive that shiny brand new car just one block from the dealership, it just lost 20% of its value. If you paid $25k for the car, just one block of driving away and it's now worth $5000 less!

Nothing I can think of depreciates faster than a new car except maybe a mobile home or electronic equipment.

But let's pile on! In addition, a new car will cost you a lot more to insure and in some states a lot more to plate!

But the biggest reason not to buy a new car is because this is one of the rare instances in life where you can have your cake and eat it!

There are always 1 year old (or even 6 month) old vehicles available "minus" the 20% of the new car. Company executives of automobile manufacturers drive new cars called "Brass Hats." When the "Brass" gets tired of driving them they give them to special dealerships to sell! Ask y our dealer if he has any "Brass Hats" for sale and you could land a big bargain. Even if he doesn't have a Brass Hat, he likely has a near new car that is just coming off lease.

Anyway, on your way to your millions you want to avoid the very expensive "new car" impulse. Your insurance will be lower, the tax you pay will be less and the early depreciation will be eaten up by whomever bought the car new.

Once you make your first million, go ahead and buy the new car if you just can't stand it.

"Anything beyond functional is ego!"

Think about this: I have a $6000 Rolex watch and you have a $20 Timex. Your watch keeps perfect time. My watch keeps perfect time. If they both keep perfect time, then you just saved $5880! Did I really need an 18k gold stainless steel watch for $6000? Of course not! Lots of ego tied up in that Rolex. If you're gonna get a million dollars, you need to check your ego.

True Story: Once, a long time ago, I pulled up at a red light on Dodge Street in Omaha, Nebraska in my brand new Mercedes Benz. Sitting right beside me in the other lane was none other than Warren Buffett driving his 10 year old Cadillac! What's wrong with *this* picture? I was so embarrassed I wanted to crawl under my seat until the light turned and he could move on. But it taught me a lesson: "Anything beyond functional is ego!" If you have a dependable vehicle with A/C in the summer and a heater in the winter, that's all you need. Today, I drive a Buick. Keep that ego in check!

The DUI (Driving Under the Influence)

What?! What does a DUI have to do with becoming a millionaire?

The answer is simple: It sets you back financially and socially a very long way!

We don't have to pay attention to the fine (which is considerable) or the attorney's fees (which are even more) but we also have the grief involved.

First, having a DUI on your record may well keep you from getting the employment you want. Maybe you're self employed? A DUI will make you pay dearly for life insurance. It will also raise your automobile insurance for the foreseeable future and not just by a little, we're talking thousands of dollars over time. Plus, it's a stigma. It will rear its ugly head at the very worst times in your life. It tells the world you can't control yourself! And it will make it infinitely more difficult to get your millions. All this 'cause you *had* to drive?

Another True Story: I knew a guy in real estate who was in line to join a group of local politicians in a development project. He stood to make millions. But in the middle of the protocol, he acquired a second DUI. It made him a political pariah. They kicked him off the board and out of the "Good Old Boy" club. Today, he struggles as a residential real estate agent.

Driving while intoxicated is just asking for a world full of trouble. You're literally playing "Misery Roulette! If you're of age, go ahead and drink. But choose to be wise enough not to take the chance of being pulled over for a DUI. And it doesn't take much. Even just two beers in less than an hour and you're probably going to breathe DUI.

We all think we're immune to getting caught. But the algorithms don't lie. Sooner or later, you'll get caught. And then things get very expensive; financially, emotionally and socially.

If you get a DUI, or if you already have one (or more), it doesn't exclude you from the Millionaire Club but it makes it just that much harder, *needlessly!*

Divorce! (The most expensive thing on earth)
Nothing, and I mean nothing, is more expensive monetarily or emotionally than divorce. Nothing

will set you back further or faster to making millions like your divorce.

If you have children with that person, add another 50% of pain. Big pain. And not just for you but for everyone involved.

Divorce will set your financial situation significantly backwards. In addition, your productivity will go down the tubes for an extended period. Even if you don't love that person anymore, it will hurt. Bad. If you've already been married and divorced you know exactly what I'm talking about. It's a long, uphill road ahead. So pay attention to the old saying: "An ounce of prevention is worth a pound of cure!" In this case meaning. choose your spouse well. Don't jump into marriage until you're as sure as you can be (and you can never be *absolutely* sure) that this is your soul mate. It will save you untold money and misery.

Unfortunately, there are times and situations where divorce is unavoidable. If this is your situation then I guess "The absence of alternatives clears the mind!" Do what you have to do. Just be sure it's a "must"

In addition, at the time you read this, you may be too young for this to be a concern. Just remember it when you're of age.

Gambling

In an interview on the news program "60 Minutes," Steve Wynn, the CEO of Wynn Resorts, a huge global gaming conglomerate, talked about individuals called "Whales." Basically, "Whales" are the highest of high rollers. They literally gamble millions, and sometimes tens of millions of dollars in his casinos. Mr. Wynn was asked by the reporter if he knew of anyone who actually won. His reply was that he couldn't think of even one individual. That's not to say that these people didn't "win" money every once in a while but eventually, they always came back to the game and lost their winnings.

Casinos work on a concept called "The Law of Long Averages." It means, the "longer" a gambler sticks around the chance he or she will lose money to the casino is near 100%

Check it out: A gambler who wins (or loses) $1000 at a blackjack table in 30 minutes and then quits playing, will have a much more difficult time getting a free meal or comp from the house than the retired lady living on social security who's playing the penny slots for hours. Even, and maybe especially if she wins! (They want her to stay so they can get their money back.)

Gambling for *entertainment*, meaning having a "fun evening" once in a while and dropping $20 or $30 bucks is no big deal. But most of us aren't able to resist the call of the stimuli in a casino. And if you stay at the party long enough, you will lose.

The casinos are full of working people. The lower your income level, the more likely you are to gamble. What's that tell you?

Gambling is a tax on the poor!

In this chapter, we've tried to show you the toll roads on your way to millions. We've pointed out the dead ends and detours.

In getting your millions, it's just as important to know what *not* to do as what you need to do to arrive at the millionaire destination. In the following chapters we'll explore the fastest and surest ways to get where you're going. They're not always the same.

Chapter 6

THE ENTREPRENEUR
THE FASTEST (LEGAL)
WAY TO WEALTH!

Let's get the facts out of the way first: Only 20% of Americans are self-employed but they make up more than two thirds of the millionaires! 23% of millionaires got that way through working for someone else. Most of them are professionals and managers.

So if you want to get your millions fast, (and who wants to get them slowly?) you should consider starting your own enterprise and/or buy a lottery ticket.

The average millionaire today is 61 years old and has a net worth of about $3 million. That's fine but

I'm pretty sure you picked up this book hoping you wouldn't have to wait 'till you're a senior citizen to enjoy your wealth.

And you don't. A business of your own can reward you financially and emotionally in just a few years but you have to do this "own your own business" thing the right way.

Here's a scary fact: 80% of startups fail within the first 18 months! Put simply, you only have a 20% chance of success. Incidentally, this counts for franchises too! Everyone thinks that franchises have a 90% success rate. They think of McDonalds and Burger King and Pizza Hut. But the dirty little secret that every franchisor (and eventually every franchisee) knows is that 80% of franchises fail as well. Buying a franchise is generally not a good idea. Here's why: There is almost always a "franchise fee." That's the money the franchisor charges you for the privilege of owning one of their franchise units. That fee can range from $5,000 to a more common $25,000 or even more, depending on the franchisor. In addition, the franchisee must usually surrender 7% of their monthly gross revenue to the franchisor, regardless of whether or not they've made a profit.

A successful business does really well if it brings a 15% net profit. If you're giving ½ of that 15% to your franchisor…well. To give you an idea: A Casino will be happy to make 4% of all the money that is wagered. A Grocery Chain is considered amazing if it delivers a 1% profit.

That surprises some people. But the reason these businesses can survive and even thrive on such low margins is simple: **Volume!**

A grocery store might have a thousand people or more visiting every day. A casino will "handle" millions of dollars every day (they'll "hold" 4% of that money on average).

But a jewelry or furniture store will make 5X what they paid for their goods. If a jewelry store pays $1000 for a diamond, they will price it at $5000 or more. That's called "Five Key." One key is 100% of the cost of goods, 5 key is 500%. The margins are even better for a furniture store. Why? Because of *volume!* A jewelry store or furniture store doesn't usually have thousands of people coming through the door every day. And if they do, they are the rare exception to the rule. Meanwhile, a jeweler may have purchased a precious gem ring years ago that's still sitting in his case. The same for that ugly orange sofa the furniture store owner bought on an off day. Businesses with small volume must have larger margins to survive.

But I digress. Let's get back to *you*! If you're going to start your own business you must be very calculating about it. If you're *very* young you could start it right out of school, if you're already in the work force it's probably a good idea to start your business "on the side" after work hours and on weekends without quitting your current job until your enterprise matures a little.

A Business You Don't Know.

You absolutely, positively do not want to get into a business you don't know or understand!

No matter what enterprise you start, you are going to make multiple mistakes in the beginning. Just count on it. And if you start a business in an industry you don't know, you are going to make many times *more* mistakes!

Almost every mistake is expensive and unexpected and you will make plenty of them your first couple of years. Don't get into something you don't know or understand and wind up making *needless* mistakes because you don't know what you're doing.

But you can eliminate many of your startup mistakes. Not all, but many. And we'll talk about that right now.

The Business Plan

The *essential*, can't do without, *don't even try without it* tool before you embark on your own business is the Business Plan. I know it's no fun and you probably don't even know where to begin to write out a formal business plan but you *must*. I can't stress enough how important this is for you. It will save you tons of money in mistakes not made and it will guide you through your toughest times. *You cannot skip your business plan!*

A formal business plan shows the world and *you* that you've thoroughly examined your business idea. That you have a *structured* plan for success. That you've considered the possible pit falls that will work against a successful outcome.

Thinking about going to a bank for a startup loan? Don't have a business plan? Forget it! The banker will ask you for it, and if you don't have one, she probably won't change her facial expression, but believe this: That banker won't respect your loan request, and your chances of obtaining that loan are very slim. If you don't have a business plan, you don't have squat. You're shooting from the hip and even cheating yourself out of likely success.

Here's the good news! It's not as difficult a project as you may think. You can go out to the Small Business Administration's web site, www.sba.gov and they will have a template you can follow to build your very own business plan. The template simply asks you important questions about your competition, barriers to entry etc. You answer the questions and when you're through it will even table the contents for you. Free!

Simply click on the SBA.Gov website and in the "search" icon at the upper right of the page. Type in the words "Business Plan Template." In addition, the SBA has counselors who will give you expert advice on starting and developing your new business at their "Small Business Development Centers." In virtually every state in the U.S. You can find the location(s) in your state at the SBA site as well.

Hopefully, you won't need to borrow money to grow your business but, if you do, borrowing from a bank is the traditional way to obtain capital for your new venture. Of course, there *are* other, better ways to raise money. You could borrow from a relative.

And don't you think mom and dad or your brother or sister would be more receptive to your request if you could show them a formal business plan?

The Private Placement Memorandum

Another way to raise money for your new venture is to sell stock in the company. This should be attempted only if you intend to grow your business into a multi-million dollar enterprise. Moreover, it's going to require some sales ability on your part.

The stock market crash of 1929 was due in part to scam artists selling stock and issuing stock certificates in companies that really didn't even exist. And so, in 1933, at the very depths of the depression, the Securities Exchange Commission (SEC) decided that some honest, ordinary folks still needed a way to raise money through selling shares in their company to more than just mom and pop.

Going "public" was (and still is) a very expensive proposition. And so the SEC decided that they'd meet us in the middle. It's called the Regulation "D" exemption or "Reg D" for short. With the filing of a "Reg D" exemption you could sell shares in your company to a limited number of individuals or entities, as long as you let the SEC know what you're doing. No more "Blue Sky" companies selling empty shares to unsuspecting investors.

The tool that you use is the "Private Placement Memorandum" or "PPM." This document must be provided to a potential investor and filed with both the SEC and the states in which you intend to secure investors. There are templates for this document that can be purchased on line but I would recommend you have it prepared by an attorney. The cost varies by law firms but $10,000 is a fair market price.

With that price tag and filing fees etc. you can see why you only want to go in this direction if your plan is to grow your company to a large, multi-million dollar enterprise in a relatively short time frame.

Generally speaking, the document will state how much money you intend to raise (usually $1,000,000) and the minimum investment you will accept. There's a lot more involved here but a conference with your attorney will educate you rather quickly and like most things on this earth, it isn't that difficult.

While you may easily raise $100k or $200k or more, there are drawbacks to this method. The biggest one is that you will now have "shareholders" and those shareholders are basically your bosses!

It's important to note here that if you're just going to sell shares to a few people, (your best friend, your brother, your mom and dad and a business associate) then a "PPM" isn't necessary. Any single digit number of investors doesn't require the "Reg D" filing. But when it gets outside your family and friends, or you have *many* friends from whom you'd look for an investment, then, it's time to put together the Private Placement.

The JOBS Act

In April of 2012 an overwhelming bipartisan majority of Congress passed the JOBS (Jumpstart Our Business Startups) act. This financial reform act was supposed to make it easier for start ups to raise money through a thing called "Crowd Funding" The problem is, like all government programs, going through the regulatory process of raising money this way is very time consuming and expensive. Actually, more expensive than using a Private Placement Memorandum. The JOBS act was even supposed to make it much easier for a start up company to go public through what is called Regulation A+ but like the Crowd Funding idea, it is very expensive and time consuming to get it done. Initial costs are somewhere around $75,000. Anyway, until they make it all much simpler, i'd just stay away from acting on these things.

There is however, another place to go to raise capital and that's funding sites like Kickstarter, or Indiegogo. Here, you just put your idea out there on the site and people can fund your idea if they like it. You have to give a reward of some kind (Like a t-shirt or coffee mug) but that's it. Some start ups have raised more than a million dollars this way.

Employees

Any small business owner who has run his or her enterprise for just a little while, will tell you that when you hire your first employee, you've just become a mom, dad and bail bondsman.

Remember this: If you pay Bob $500 a week, that's not where it ends. You are also required by law to match his or her social security to the current tune of 7.5% which would be an additional $37.50 per week. Plus, you'll have to purchase workman's comp insurance and unemployment contributions. Both of which will be at least hundreds of dollars a year. So, the economic reality is that you're actually paying your new employee about $600 per week. Hold off as long as you can from hiring an employee.

Partners

Nope! No Partners! Everyone wants to start a business with a partner. It's a comfort. Makes you feel like you're splitting the risk. But for most of us the only thing you're splitting is your friendship.

Partnerships don't last, and a partnership started with a friend is a sure fire way to lose a friend. In fact, it's a very good way to make a new enemy. Sooner or later (and probably sooner) one of you will feel like the other isn't pulling their end of the train. Maybe you won't say anything at first. But the emotional baggage will accumulate and things will end up very badly.

To be fair, like any rule, there are exceptions. Just like there are people who actually *do* win the lottery. It just isn't likely to be you.

If you just can't make yourself listen to me in this matter, then at least have an attorney draw up what is called a "Buy/Sell" agreement. It's sometimes called a "Drop Dead Buy Sell Agreement" because it's also possible that a co-owner may actually drop dead!

Then what? If you have a Buy/Sell Agreement, you've taken care of what could have otherwise been a real dilemma.

Beyond that, it actually sets out a plan if an eventual split up occurs. Ideally, this document should be in place before you start your partnership.

This concept usually has a life insurance policy tied to it to insure the surviving party can pay to "buy out" the other co-owners interest.

Alright! Let's say that despite the warnings, you *have* to have a partner! In that case, at least give me this:

Do not, under any circumstances, go into a 50/50 partnership!

That is the kiss of death for both of you. If you *do* go into a partnership then know this: You are better off having 49% than 50%.

At least then somebody is going to be able to make a decision.

When I was a very young man, I went into a 50/50 partnership with another fellow. We happily set things up so that it took both of our signatures for a check to be valid. After a while there was a conflict. Sooner or later all relationships have conflicts. In this case, neither of us would sign a check for anything.

Nothing got paid. Not even us. My co-owner eventually left the business after causing a lot of grief with efforts to hinder the future success of the business. It was just hurtful. The experience was very similar to a bad divorce. To this day (40 years later) we speak to each other on rare occasions but we are no longer friends. It is so tempting, especially when you're young, to want a partner in your new venture. But any banker will validate what I've told you here. Partnerships don't last and usually end up with bad feelings on both sides. There's 3 sides to every ending of a partnership story: Her side, your side, and what really happened.

Chapter 7

FIRST WE SAVE, THEN WE INVEST!

In the last chapter, I told you the "fastest" (legal) way to make millions is to start your own business. That holds true. But even the *word* "Entrepreneur" loosely translated in French, means "Risk Taker." There is no doubt that the fastest way also carries the most risk.

So what if you're not cut out for all that risk? Does this mean you don't get to be a millionaire? Absolutely not! In fact, you likely have a *better* chance than the entrepreneur! The fastest way isn't always the *surest* way. Just ask the Tortoise and the Hare!

If you approach your millionaire status in a structured, long term, low risk, almost passive fashion; you've taken most of the "chance" out of your journey.

Pay Yourself First!

I'm not the originator of this concept. It was defined a long time ago but it is the surest fire way of accumulating wealth. I'm sure you already know what it means but allow me to describe the process for you.

Before you invest, you want to save. And the way you save, is by paying yourself first. Take a percentage of your income (whatever it is) large or small, and look at it like a car payment or a utility payment. 15% of your income would be ideal but even if it's only 5% you're doing the right thing. If you "clear" just $400 a week and you pay yourself just $20 (5%) of that money, I contend that you won't miss it, even if you're living paycheck to paycheck (which you probably are).

Each of us, no matter our income, throws away at least $20 a week on something. And the beauty of this "Pay Yourself First" concept is that *you still have the money*! In fact, it's accumulating! If an emergency comes along that money is there for you. Instead of throwing it away on some vaporous (what's that mean?) comfort, you have access to it. And at $400 a week salary, in just *two months* you have $160 "extra" cash. If you make more, then it's that much better!

If I offered you $160 instead of 5 extra "twinkies" a week for two months wouldn't you rather have the $160? Well, that *is* what I'm offering you! And guess what! Now you only need $999,840.00 to get to your million! You've done that in just two months!

If you continue this "petty cash" savings plan you will notice in short order that you have a little more financial peace of mind. Some breathing room if an emergency develops. But to get an invite to the millionaire club you must pay yourself as much money as possible every single week. Once again, remember: *You still have the money!* It's just not being spent.

So you pay yourself before you pay any other bill. An amount, of course, that's not going to keep you from paying your other bills. You want to keep a good credit (FICO) score or work very hard to fix a poor credit score and here's the primary reason why: *"As long as you have good credit, you're never broke!"*

Good credit shows character. Character is defined as *"The ability to carry out the promise, after the mood of the promise is over."* We all have lapses of discipline at times. If this is where you are, then you have to fix it at your earliest opportunity. You *do* want that million dollars, don't you?

The younger you are, the better. Time is surely the most valuable commodity. But if you're middle aged or even older, we can still get there.

One more item in this savings plan I should mention. You want to put the money where it will be "inconvenient" to get to it. Maybe a piggy bank that you have to smash open to get to the money or maybe a savings account with no minimum so you have to go to the bank to access the cash. "Out of sight, out of mind."

There are many different ways to save but save you must in order to begin to "invest." Unless we already have a significant cash position, we save first, we invest later.

The 52 week money challenge

You may have already heard of this project. It's believed to have been originated in 2013 through a Facebook group called "Kassondra's 52-week Money Challenge," created by Kassondra Perry-Moreland. It makes saving money more fun. The idea goes like this: Week 1 you save just $1. Week two you save $2. Week 3 you save $3 etc. until week 52 you would save $52 and when your year is up you'll have saved $1,378.

However, a lot depends on when during the year you begin! If you begin in December, that's ok for the first year 'cause you're only saving $1. But at the end of the year it's Christmas time and you may not be able to save $52!

So, you might want to do the reverse 52 week challenge. Begin in January with $52 then February $51 and so on until after 12 months your last payment is just $1. But always keep in mind that you want to make your savings "inconvenient" to get to or you'll be tempted to take and spend it. You could also double the money you save and after a year you have $2756. Nice!

The Health Savings Plan (HSA)
You know how the big shots keep dodging taxes? Well, you have that opportunity right at your fingertips as well. It's a building block and good training for when you become a millionaire big shot too!. You just have to pay attention.

Are you going to buy a pair of glasses anytime soon? Cough medicine? Antacids? Then you need to open a Health Savings Account. Why? Because if you don't you're just leaving money on the sidewalk.

Your health insurance isn't going to pay for your new glasses or contacts. So you have to pay your own money. Well, since you're buying those things anyway, open up a Health Savings Account (HSA) at a bank near you! It's easy and free at most banks and takes about 10 minutes!

The money you put in that HSA is the same money you were going to spend on those new glasses and eye exam anyway. But now it's tax deductible! There's no minimum amount you can contribute (though there is a maximum) Look at it this way. If you put just $500 in the HSA and you're in just the 25% tax bracket, the IRS is going to let you deduct that $500 right off the top even if you don't spend it! That's a cool extra $125 back on your income tax refund. Put in $1000 that's $250 more back on taxes! If you save that extra $250 "gift" from your government and combine it with the $160 you saved a couple of pages ago, you only have to find $999,590.00 more to get your first million.

Sounds daunting I know but look how fast and easy you whittled $410 off that million! And it's money you were gonna spend anyway! You just put it in a different place before you spent it! Now you pay for the glasses out of your tax deductible HSA account!

Or, you can just pay for your new glasses yourself and that's the same as standing in the parking lot throwing $125 - $250 cash into the wind.

Compound Interest

When I write about "compound interest" I'm not reporting any breaking news here. Einstein purportedly said: *"The most powerful force on earth is compound interest!"* And if you could get an audience with Warren Buffett he'd probably tell you that a great measure of his success in investing was tied to compound interest.

At its base, the concept isn't very complicated. It's simply accumulating interest on the interest you've already been paid.

So if you invest $10,000 at a simple 5% interest, you will have $10,500 at the end of a year. You can pick up your $500 profit and move on. But if you keep the investment, and it keeps paying the 5%, interest will now be paid on your initial $10,000 plus interest on the $500 you earned. So in year two your investment will be worth $11,025. By the end of year three it will be worth $11,576.25. In 3 years, you've made 1,576.25 by doing virtually nothing but "let it ride!"

But where do you find 5% on your money in 2015? Certainly not at a bank!

Today, banks *brag* about giving you 2% on a 3 year CD. For comparison, back in 1980, some bank certificates of deposit were paying 17% per annum! I won't go into why that happened, except to say that runaway inflation had a lot to do with it.

Anyway, you're not going to get 5% from a bank CD anytime soon. And remember this; when your CD term expires, you have just 10 days to get your money or it automatically renews!

Quick! If a bank pays you 2% for your savings account, how long will it take you to double your money?

Answer: 36 years!

The quick answer is available through a mathematical concept called "The rule of 72." Simply divide whatever interest rate you receive by the number 72 and you have the answer. i.e. 10% interest will take 7.2 years to double your money. As an exercise, you may want to take the rule of 116! That's the triple your money rule! Divide your interest rate into 116 and that's how long it will take to triple your money. Anyway, we can't wait 36 years for our money to double so to accumulate real wealth, eventually, we're going to have to invest!

Chapter 8

TIME TO INVEST!

To begin, let's be clear: *There is no such thing as a "risk free investment!* You can even lose money with U.S. Treasuries!

That being said, once you have accumulated a modest amount of money through saving, you should begin to invest. *But not on your own.* If you start investing in assets based on your own judgment, you are like the kid who buys a football one day and tries out for the Green Bay Packers the next. You're gonna fail.

The first place to look for investing is your current job. Many employers have a 401K program for their employees. Some will match whatever you put into your 401k account up to 6% of your income. If you have this available and you don't take *full* advantage of it, consider yourself unwise. There are few, if any investments you can take today that will give you a 100% return. But an employer "match" will do that immediately!

There is nowhere else on this planet where you can get a guaranteed 100%. And we haven't even looked into the money you get deducted from your taxes! You *have* to do this for the full amount you're allowed. I know it's hard and it feels like you're taking a cut in pay but this is one great start toward your millions! However, many companies don't offer a 401K match or even a 401K.

In that instance, you have to put the maximum you're allowed into an IRA. If you don't, it's the same as throwing money on the sidewalk. You have to keep in mind all the time that you're not "spending or losing" the money you put in your IRA. *It's still your money!* If you get in a bind you can have it back and no one can keep you from it! (There is a 10% penalty if you take it before 59 ½ *but it's still your money*, available to you whenever you want it!) And you get a tax deduction too! Whew!

There are several types of IRAs. In a Traditional IRA you deposit the money in a Stock Brokerage account, Mutual Fund, Bank CD, Gold, Rare Art, many things. The money or precious metal you put in is deducted from your tax bill. It can be substantial.

If you put $3000 in an IRA, and you're in just the 25% tax bracket, your tax refund is going to be $750 larger! And you still have your $3000! You just made $750 *cash* and your investment hasn't even started to grow yet!

In a "Roth" IRA you pay the taxes on the $3000 (or whatever sum) before you put it in the IRA. (but you still get the deduction) But any money that grows in your IRA will NEVER be taxed again. So if you make $50,000 over the life of your Roth IRA, when you take it out, you pay no tax on the profit. None. Ever. With a traditional IRA, when you withdraw the money, you'll be taxed at your regular rate at the time.

In summary, your 401K or IRA, whatever type you choose is your FIRST INVESTMENT. Every other investment comes after you put the full amount you're legally allowed into these programs. It is literally "free money" and in some cases a 100% return.

You don't have to be an investment wizard for these. Most 401k's give you a choice of which Mutual Fund to put your money. With traditional IRAs it's a little trickier. My best advice is to open a brokerage account and buy a high rated Mutual Fund.

If you've never done it before, believe me, it's as easy as ordering pizza. Just call a TD Ameritrade, E-Trade, Scottrade or any online broker and they'll help you. You don't (in fact you shouldn't) need a financial advisor for your IRA. I'll explain why in later pages.

INSURANCE

I can't think of any scenario where buying Insurance will make you wealthy. In fact, its very name tells you that! "Insurance!" It's meant to "insure" your wealth not generate wealth. For this reason, as a general rule, you want to purchase a product called "Term" insurance and not "Whole Life" or "Universal Life"

In addition, If you have a family, it's probably necessary to purchase insurance but if you're young and single, don't bother. Your money will be better spent somewhere else. Think of it this way: You don't purchase insurance for *you*, you purchase it for the benefit of your *survivors*.

If a life insurance agent keeps pushing you to purchase "Whole Life" he or she is probably more interested in their commission than your future financial well being.

Simply put, buying insurance is not investing. An insurance agent may try to argue that point but it has no merit. Let's take their "Whole Life" insurance product. The agent may tell you that you will accumulate "cash value" inside the insurance policy.

But the agent won't dwell on the fact that "Whole Life" costs as much as 5 times the premium of "Term" and that when you *do* accumulate cash value, after many years, that you can have it "if" you "borrow" your cash value from your policy.

Know what that means? First, your cash value will be paltry compared to what you've paid in premiums. Second, why should you have to "borrow" money from your own cash value? The Agent may say: "Well, you don't really have to pay the money back if you take the cash value out" That's true. However, the face value of your policy will be worth less! Here's an example. Let's say you take out a $100,000 whole life policy. After paying 5 years worth of premiums it has a "cash value" of $1500. You need the money so you decide to "borrow" against your policy. Fine.

And you don't have to pay it back. However, the face value of your policy is now just $98,500. $100,000 minus the $1500 your borrowed?

There's an old saying that goes like this: "They didn't build those big beautiful casinos with people's winnings!" When it comes to insurance companies, the same applies. They didn't build those towering skyscraper headquarters by paying out premiums!

Think of this: If you pay a yearly life insurance premium of just $1200 ($100 per month) and you stay alive; that $1200 is pure gross profit other than administrative costs and commissions. And speaking of commissions, for many insurance agents, the first year commission on a Whole Life policy can be as high as 90% of the premium! You pay a $3000 premium, the agent gets $2700 of it in commission. Commissions on "Term" life are much lower. Wonder why? 96% of life insurance policies are never paid to beneficiaries!

That's not to say insurance companies don't pay on the policy if they are legally obligated, just that most policies expire for various reasons before the individual passes on. In summary, you should consider insurance if the "need" arises but *buying insurance is not investing.*

ANNUITIES

This is yet another insurance company product. And while annuities are an investment vehicle, by and large they aren't very good ones. One of the tell tell signs of a questionable investment is the commission rate paid to the agent.

Insurance companies pay big commissions to agents selling annuities. That's because as time goes by, there are lots of profit for the insurance company as well.

Now, if the agent and the insurance company are making such large profits, what's left for you the purchaser? Does *everybody* make money? Well, perhaps but you won't make what you could in many other investment vehicles. In addition, your annuity purchase is tied up at least for 5 years and usually for a lot longer. If you "cash out" early, you'll pay a hefty penalty.

To accumulate real wealth, we have to look elsewhere. I cannot think of one good reason to purchase an annuity, at least not while you're young and maybe never.

STOCKS, BONDS AND MUTUAL FUNDS

Until you have $10,000 in cash to invest, the best way for you to go is to invest in a Mutual Fund. As a general rule Mutual Funds are managed by individuals who are awesome in what they do. Particularly large funds like Fidelity and Vanguard. They won't designate an individual as a manager until she's proven herself to know her way around the world of investments.

Moreover, a Mutual Fund is diversified. Literally the first rule of investing: "Diversification"! The Mutual Fund you invest in is likely to have 20 or more holdings so your risk is spread out among many different securities. But how do you choose which Mutual Fund to give your money? Well, a lot of that depends on its past history, its current rating and the fees they charge.

Remember when I said earlier that you don't necessarily need a financial advisor? That's because when you're first starting out the cost of a financial advisor is too steep. Usually (but not always) they are paid a commission called a 12b1 fee from the Mutual Funds they sell you.

It's called a 12b1 fee after the 12b1 law allowing a fund to commission the Financial Advisor for recommending a certain Mutual Fund, regardless of its track record.

Let me explain: In regards to fees, there are basically two types of Mutual Funds: Load, and No Load. Substitute the word "Load" for commission and you have idea of what I'm talking about.

"Loaded Mutual Funds" have fees. Some have fees up front to get in, some have back end fees when you exit and some have both! In addition, they have management fees! It can all be expensive! With "No Load" Funds, you literally pay nothing to get in or out, though you do pay a management fee.

Seldom will a Financial Advisor recommend you purchase a "no load" fund because there's no commission for him or her. Beyond that, over all, "no load" funds perform just as well as "loaded" funds.

Curiously though, people who invest in "loaded" funds do better than those who invest in "no load" funds. Can you guess why? It's because there is no penalty for cashing out of "no load" funds and so people "chase money" buying and selling no loads and moving on.

As a general rule, you're better off buying a "no load" fund and avoiding the commissions *if* you stay with the fund long enough for it to reward you for your patience.

How do you find a "no load" fund? Simply Google "no load funds" and you'll find all you want. In addition, they'll probably be rated on a 1 to 5 stars by a company called "Morningstar" the good ones will publicize their 4 or 5 star ratings while the poor ones won't mention it. So, stay away from the poorly rated. Duh!

You can purchase a Mutual Fund through an online broker or direct from the Mutual Fund company. Either way, it won't cost you much. The Broker will only charge you about $10 for your purchase. Just like individual stocks, Mutual Funds have a symbol, usually 5 letters. You can find their symbol with your on line broker simply by typing the name of the Mutual Fund and clicking on the "Search Symbol" icon; or you can call your broker and ask for the symbol of any given Mutual Fund. They'll be happy to accommodate you.

Mutual Funds, loaded or not, price themselves at the end of the daily market close.

You can't buy or sell your Mutual Fund until the end of the trading day because the Fund doesn't know its' worth until they tally up the net worth of all their assets at the end of the day. They then come up with the Fund's "Net Asset Value" or NAV, and that's the price you pay to buy or the price you get to sell.

There are also Mutual Funds called "Exchange Traded Funds" or ETFs. These funds are actually traded on the New York Stock Exchange or NASDAQ and trade just like stocks. Generally, these "ETFs" are geared toward certain "sectors" like Oil, Industrials, or even stocks in foreign countries. ETFs operate like traditional Mutual Funds. There are no loads but there are management fees which are variable.

Anyway, as with all Mutual Funds, some do very well for their investors and some do very poorly. I won't mention which are which in this book as their performance could change and it's good for you to do your own research which is easy to acquire on-line. As with Mutual Funds, ETFs have their own symbols on the exchanges.

DOLLAR COST AVERAGING

One of the smartest and most profitable ways to invest in Mutual Funds (or any equity for that matter) is to utilize a concept called "Dollar Cost Averaging." The process is easy enough to apply and it goes like this:

In regular intervals, (once a week, once a month etc.) you invest the same amount of money into your mutual fund. Doesn't matter what the amount of money is as long as it is the same as the previous investment.

When you do this, you are purchasing more shares when the fund's price is lower and fewer shares when the fund's price is higher.

i.e. If you invest $100 today and the price of one share of the Mutual Fund is $10, you're buying 10 shares. But next month (or week) when you invest $100 again, one share of the Mutual Fund maybe $8! Then you'll get more for your money. You'll get 12 .5 shares for that same $100.

Purchasing in intervals like this is not "risk free" because nothing is, but it mitigates (another big word) much of the risk of buying too many shares at too high a price!

BONDS

When you're trying to accumulate wealth, bonds aren't going to be your investment of choice; at least not in the current environment.

Bonds are an "income" investment, not a growth investment. They're (sometimes) good for a retiree who has already made their money and just wants a good, steady income.

Going back again to 1981, bonds were a good idea because they would pay double digit returns. But today, bonds do little better than banks which is paltry.

Some bonds, called "High Yield Bonds" will pay as much as 6% in today's economic environment.

But there's always a reason. When you hear the term "Junk Bonds" that's the same as "High Yield Bonds." The term was coined in the late 1980's when a fellow named "Michael Milkie" used "High Yield Bonds" as collateral for leverage.

As a general rule, the higher the interest rate paid, the greater the risk that the issuer of the bond will default and leave the investor with nothing. Hence the term: "Junk Bonds."

Anyway, bonds are mostly for income, not growth, so we're not going to go down that road on our map. No bonds, let's look at the stock market.

THE STOCK MARKET

Now, here's where you have a chance to make real money if you do it correctly. But correctly can be complicated. It's why I recommend Mutual Funds first. Then, after you have an "awareness" of how the market works, you can begin to buy individual stocks. There are some rules.

If you get frisky and decide that one or more of the rules don't apply to you, then get ready to lose piles of money. They apply to you and almost everyone else.

In today's society, we call dead cow meat a hamburger or a steak. Why don't we call it what it is? Dead Cow Meat! Because very few people would eat it or order it at the restaurant if we called it what it is.

In the stock market we're buying the shares of "companies." But we don't call them companies; we call them "stocks" or "securities." This can lead you astray to forgetting you're buying a company just like you tend to forget a hamburger is dead cow meat.

So… the rules:

* **Buy companies not stocks!** Find out what the company does. Look at its fundamentals. It's all available to you at the touch of a Google search engine.
* **Buy and hold!** (most of the time). Prepare to stay with whatever you buy for the foreseeable future or even, as Warren Buffett would say: "Forever"
* **Don't buy Penny Stocks!** Shares priced under $5 are called Penny Stocks. As a general rule, *don't buy Penny Stocks!* There's a reason they're priced so low and though you can buy gobs of shares in these companies for little money, you can also purchase cow manure

pretty inexpensively as well. Do you want cow manure at any price???

* **Buy shares in "Blue Chip" and/or "Growth"** companies with strong fundamentals and possibly a strong track record of dividends.

* **"Pigs get fat, Hogs get Slaughtered!"** (Just in case, I'll elaborate on this one later)

* **Don't act on a stock "tip"** If someone gives you a stock tip, no matter how good it sounds, stay away! It's probably bogus, and even if it has merit, by the time the waiter at the restaurant gives you the tip, it's already too late. However, there is a difference between a stock "tip" and a stock "pick" by a professional. Just "tip" the waiter and forget his tip,

* **Use an online, discount broker.** The full service broker you call on the phone (or calls YOU on the phone) likely doesn't have much more experience than you. He's probably just passed a test he crammed for to get his broker's license. Senior stock brokers seldom make cold calls. In addition, he will charge you at least $150 to $250 to make your trade. Do it on line yourself and it costs you $9.99. (In some on-line brokerages, just $5.)

These are just some of the "base" rules. There are dozens more nuances in market trading that only experience will teach you. However, following these will give you a very good foundation to begin trading.

So, let's talk about the "why" in some of these rules. I think you'll find it fascinating.

When you purchase shares in a company, there are many fundamentals to consider before you pull the trigger. I feel the most important is "Price to Sales" or P/S. The lower this number the better. If the Price to Sales is 1x or lower, you have a great number going for you. The reason is, the price relative to their revenue is very low. If you're bringing in sales, you're bringing in profits. In addition you want to pay attention to the "Price to Earnings" or P/E. Again, the lower the number the better. A P/E of 11x earnings or below is perfect. However, "average" P/E's are different for different sectors of the economy. For instance, the average P/E's for the Health Care sector is currently 24x whereas for the Financial Sector the average is 14x Free cash flow is also important. How much free cash flow does the company have?

Meanwhile, the most important item you need to know is "What does this company do?" I can't tell you how many times I've heard people talking about a "stock" they bought but have no idea what the company does. It seems silly that an individual would buy shares in a company but have no idea what the company does. But it's more common than you might think. This is usually the result of someone getting a "tip" from someone and acting on it. Bad idea. Basically, it's the same as going into Walmart with a blind fold on and purchasing an item having no idea what it was, just because someone told you it was "on sale!"

In conclusion, there are many different elements of a company you can inquire before you buy. Most of the terminology will be explained in the online brokers website if you don't understand them. (E-trade is particularly good at this). But please understand, "trading" in stocks is best reserved for professionals. "Investing" in companies is best for you. Just pick wisely and then hold on. If you choose quality companies, it won't matter much to you what happens to the stock market on a daily basis.

That brings me to the point of "Penny Stocks" vs. "Blue Chips." As I explained earlier, Penny Stocks are those that are priced less than $5 a share. Blue Chips are shares in companies that have strong fundamentals and sometimes even pay dividends bigger than a bank is willing to pay you for a CD.

It's tempting for a new investor to put money into a Penny Stock. After all, you could spend $1000 on a .10 cent Penny Stock and own 10,000 shares! What would happen if that stock went up to just a $1??? Well, you'd make $10,000! But that's not likely to happen. That same $1000 into a $100 Blue Chip Stock will only buy you 10 lousy shares! What are going to do with that?

Well, the truth is, the "lousy" shares are the 10,000 ten cent shares and the ten Blue Chip shares are golden!

Think of the two companies as real estate. The Penny Stock you purchase is land you invested in down in the worst part of the city. The ghetto. The land might be worth a lot one day a long time from now but even that is a stretch. The 10 shares you bought in the Blue Chip are in a gated community with parks and upscale shopping malls etc. That land is only going to appreciate in value.

Which one would be easier to sell when the time comes? And which one is likely to be worth more when it's time to sell? That's not to say that "some" Penny Stocks aren't worth looking at but not for you. They are best left to the people who trade them for a living.

Millionaires don't buy Penny Stocks. You're going to be a millionaire so you can't buy them either. Sorry.

But don't mistake "Growth Stocks" for Penny Stocks. A good growth stock may not even have any earnings (like the early days of Facebook) but as the company grows so does the value of its shares. If you want to make millions in the market, you're going to need some growth stocks in your portfolio.

Speaking of "selling," there is a time when everything gets sold. Your grandfather's farm, the home you live in, whatever the asset, there is a time to sell it. Your investment portfolio is like that. If you have shares in a company that has delivered a huge return, (20% or more) you may want to consider selling off at least ½ of your holdings in that company. Why? Because nothing goes straight up without coming down. You can always buy back into it later when it settles. Remember the warning: *"Pigs get fat, Hogs get slaughtered!"*

REAL ESTATE

> *"Buy real estate! They're not making*
> *any more of the stuff!"*
> *Will Rogers*

Probably more millionaires have been made through real estate dealings than any other endeavor. But it's a long road to go as real estate will usually take its time appreciating. But there are many ways to generate immediate cash flow in real estate. Rental properties, farm land, storage units and more. We'll explore them all in later pages.

The first question most people ask about purchasing real estate is: "Should I buy a home?" And the best answer is: "maybe!" In past decades you could count on your home appreciating 8% per year. That's a sweet return but it's not the situation anymore. The housing bubble and subsequent housing crises of 2008 kind of put a lid on the appreciation of homes. Suddenly people found themselves owing more than their homes were worth. No longer could you count on the 8% per year appreciation.

To be fair, housing has rebounded somewhat in the past 2 years but it's still a long way from the wonderfulness home ownership was in the past. Beyond appreciation, home ownership requires thousands of dollars of expenses that offset the appreciation. Taxes, Insurance, utilities, lawn mowers, snow blowers, landscaping, maintenance, repairs, upgrades etc.

While it's true you'll pay utility bills in an apartment, they'll be a fraction of your homeowner utilities. Most apartments are insulated on at least 3 sides and some on the roof and flooring as well. A $200 electric bill in a single family dwelling looks like $75 in an apartment of the same size. Meanwhile, someone else is mowing the lawn, clearing the snow, repairing your appliances, paying the taxes and insurance, and maintaining the property. The landlord works for you when you rent an apartment.

Moreover, the tax and interest deduction you get when you own a home is on average, a negligible $582 per year. It's certainly not the reason to buy a home.

Still, there are advantages to home ownership. Maybe just the privacy alone is worth the extra expense. If you have children, a home is most likely a better environment to grow up in than an apartment. Plus, there should be at least *some* appreciation in your home over time.

Rental Properties

How about this: You live in an apartment and you start investing in rental properties! You purchase a modest single family dwelling or duplex and your tenants pay enough rent for you to get a "cash flow!"

That means the rent they pay is more than your mortgage payment on that property. Plus, the tax breaks for you are many and varied. Pick up 5 or 6 properties like that over a few years and you've got a nice, solid income. It's not that difficult to do. The bank will help you. Start with one and then expand. Most of your properties will appreciate, every month the mortgages get paid down, you've got tax breaks all over the place and maybe one day you wind up building an entire apartment complex!

You're making money while you're sleeping!

Speaking of sleeping, there are some drawbacks to the rental property business. Like the apartment dweller, your renter doesn't want to fix that toilet that clogged up at 2 a.m.! Somebody (you) has to come over and fix things. In addition, many renters will do significant damage to your property far beyond the small security deposit they paid you. And, of course, some will stiff you on the rent and move out in the middle of the night. Some won't even bother to do that! They'll skip the rent and force you to evict them. And so, as you expand your property holdings you'll eventually need a handyman, attorney, and expenses like new carpeting, paint, etc. to make your damaged properties suitable for the next tenant.

Commercial Real Estate

An investment in commercial real estate is best left to real estate professionals. To begin, it takes an enormous amount of capital and generally a lot of bank leverage.

However, you can get a piece of the commercial real estate pie through the stock market by investing in Real Estate Investment Trusts (REITS).

Before we get into investing in REITS, I want to stress once again that there is no such thing as a "risk free" investment! I bring this up because REITS can appear to be risk free because of their high total returns. It's quite common to get double digit dividends from REITS. Sometimes as high a 20% or more! The reason is this:

By law, Real Estate Investment Trusts (REITS) must pay out at least 90% of their taxable income to shareholders in the form of dividends.

A Real Estate Investment Trust is a company that owns and operates income producing real estate. REITS own many kinds of commercial real estate, from office and apartment buildings to warehouses, shopping centers, hotels etc. REITS were designed to provide a real estate investment structure similar to the structure mutual funds provide for investments in stocks. Today, you can actually own a piece of a strip mall for as little as $4 bucks.

You purchase REITS in the stock market like any other listed security. And, like any Mutual fund or individual stock, there are good REITS and bad. You need to investigate the net asset value (NAV) and funds from operation (FFO) of any REIT before buying their stock.

The price of an individual REIT can go up or down just like any other security, and that's how you can lose money with a REIT purchase. The dividend can also go up or down depending on the market. In any event, REITS are one way for you to become a commercial property developer with just a small investment.

Some REITS listed on stock exchanges are "American Capital Agency" (Symbol AGNC) and Armour Residential (Symbol ARR) At the time of this writing, AGNC sells for around $20 a share and pays a 12.36% dividend. ARR also sells for about $20 a share and pays a 19.79% dividend. Sounds great huh? Just remember, those dividends could fall precipitously (another 5 dollar word) and the price of your shares could fall as well.

Farmland

This is a long term investment and takes a tremendous amount of capital. But it also produces income and, if one can withstand the ups and downs of the market, it will eventually provide you with significant asset wealth. Unless your family is already invested in farmland, this is probably an unattainable asset for you until you've accumulated a high net worth.

Storage Units and Mobile Home Parks

I don't think you'll find this category in any other financial book but these ventures are really worth looking into. You buy a piece of land and you put up storage units! Or, you do the same only with mobile home parking on your slabs. Trust me, this is big money and it can sustain you till you die. Think of it! $40 a month to store your belongings in a 10X12 garage like container. No maintenance, no toilets to clean, no muss, no fuss. You just collect the rent every month. Same thing with a mobile home park. You just pour a cement slab and they park the Mobile Home on top of it. "$400+ a month please!" Maintenance etc. is up to the home owner. They stop paying rent?

You kick them out of the park or sell their home or both.

I'm not saying there aren't any headaches in this set up. There are always problems when you run a business of any kind. Expenses you never expected, problem clients and employees and on and on and on. It's just the nature of business. But it's all worthwhile if your margins are adequate.

Precious Metals

Few very wealthy individuals invest much of their portfolio in precious metals. That being said, there are investors who have made millions and even billions in gold in the last 15 years. In May of 2001, the price of an ounce of gold was $286.16. By August of 2011 the price was $1,921.17 an ounce. Today, (2015) an ounce of gold sells for about $1,100. Some analysts say it will rise to $5000 an ounce, others predict it will fall to the low hundreds again. Today, the price of silver generally follows the price of gold up or down and is often called "The poor man's gold" because it can be bought for a fraction of the cost of an ounce of gold. We can also look at platinum (which is more expensive than gold) and other metals like palladium.

Commodities

Copper, platinum, gold, silver, pork bellies, feeder cattle, corn, oats, coffee etc. are all "commodities" of a sort. The best advice I can give you on trading futures contracts on any commodity is *"Don't do it."* It is best left to professional traders. It's best to just pretend the market doesn't exist. You're literally better off flying to Las Vegas and throwing dice.

Chapter 9

WHERE TO INVEST????

You can be a millionaire simply by saving money. But you will be a wealthy individual much faster by investing wisely. As you've seen, there are many asset classes of investments to choose from and it would be near impossible to list all of them in this book. There are rare coins, gems, stamps, art, collectibles etc. just to name a few more. But the assets we've described in the previous chapters are the "Main Stream" investments.

It's important to understand what is a *realistic* return. A 10% annual return on investment (ROI) makes you a "crackerjack" investor. Berkshire Hathaway, the flagship of legendary investor Warren Buffett, is arguably the most appreciated stock in the market today. One share sells for $200,000 plus. From 2000 to 2012, Berkshire appreciated 120%. Terrific! But remember, that's 10% per year. That' doesn't mean you can't hit a "home run" in the market. There are mutual funds that have delivered as much as 30% and more in the recent past but home runs with investments are like home runs in baseball, they don't come with every swing of the bat.

Still, you can and should expect an occasional home run if you diversify your investments well into quality holdings. In fact, you *must* have at least a few home runs to win the wealth contest. Somewhere along the way, you're going to have to step up to the plate and swing for the fences. The secret is to swing at the right pitch.

In your lifetime, you are going to have maybe 5 or 6 opportunities to really knock the financial ball out of the park. One or two of those have probably already come and gone. You either didn't recognize them or they just didn't feel right. That's ok. Nobody gets 'em all.

You could invest in a "start up" company. Something or someone you believe in. But you have to know these are the highest risk dollars you'll ever invest. However, it's also possible the next Bill Gates is living next to you working on the beginnings of Microsoft. There's a story about Kevin Plank, the founder of Under Armour. It was 1996 and 23 year old Kevin Plank was looking for $10,000 investments in his new company. No one seemed interested. Had they invested $10,000 in Mr. Plank's company in 1996, it would be worth $144,000,000 today! I have no idea if the story is true but the numbers are accurate.

23 year old Kevin Plank started Under Armour in the basement of his Grandmother's home. So, maybe the next Steve Jobs is working in the garage next door to you. Or maybe *you're* the next Steve Jobs! You just have to keep your eyes open and *recognize* the opportunities that surround you.

At any given time, there are literally thousands of million dollar plus opportunities right under our noses. They're right here in front of us right now but they're hidden from plain view like those puzzles when you were a kid that said "Can you find the puppies in this picture?" They'd be hidden in trees and bushes etc.

I'll give you a real life example of an opportunity sitting under our noses for years until someone saw the "pot of gold" hidden in the tree trunk. "Fantasy Football" has been around for years. Participants would pay a fee and compete against each other in fantasy leagues by managing real players or position units from real NFL teams. At the end of the season, the man or woman who picked the best team of players would win the league season and maybe a cash prize from the pool of a few hundred dollars.

Then, in 2012, a couple of executives of "Vista Print" figured out that there could be big money in doing "daily" and "weekly" fantasy teams in MLB, NHL, NFL, the NBA and PGA. Because winning required skill rather than just chance, it was considered legal wagering. You pay a fee, pick your players or units in the sport of your choice and you could a million dollars or more. Plus, you didn't have to wait for a season to come and go, you could pay a fee every day. The winners could literally win millions! The company is called Draft Kings®

Here it was, just a new angle on Fantasy Football which was sitting there all along. In 3 short years it's grown to a multi-billion dollar company and Major League Baseball has invested in it. Can you find the puppy in the tree trunk? Believe this: He's there!

It can be very tempting to invest in a "start up" but the money invested should never be anything but disposable dollars. If you lost all of your investment (and it's very likely you will) and losing it would change your lifestyle; the home you live in, the car you drive, the vacation you could have taken, then don't even consider it and don't ask anyone else in that situation.

Speculation vs. Investing

To the untrained eye, these two may look the same but they're nothing alike. Let's look at the difference. Pretend for a moment that you started a business. Pick the business you want but let's begin with a small restaurant. Ok. You invest $20k with a friend who is the principal owner of the enterprise. Your agreement with him is that you can sell back your interest any time you choose at the fair market value at the time you decide to sell.. After three months the restaurant is wildly popular and everybody who invested is tripping over their wallets. You approach the principal and tell him you want to sell your interest. This is *speculation!* It sure looks like you invested but because you made your exit in just 90 days you eliminated the other part of investing: Time! It's not always a bad idea to speculate but it's a bad idea if you don't realize you're doing it. Back in the late 1990's there was a group of individuals called "Day Traders" these guys would trade millions of shares of stock every day and close out their positions by the close of the market. Some made money. Most did not. Yes, they were purchasing stock in companies but this was by no means investing. It was speculation, pure and simple. Not always, but almost always, making money in the short term is "speculation" and it's a much more expensive way to make money. Why? First, the government punishes you for making money quickly. The tax you pay on your profit is taxed the same as your income. (Which, is currently 39.6% for upper income individuals) If you wait a year or more to take your profits they'll be taxed at a much lower rate. (Usually 15%) In 2015, I would contend that there is no one who is day trading successfully. Not just because of the high tax rates on profits but also because the risk is very high in speculation. You have to give a good investment "time" to cook. If you keep going for the "get rich quick" speculation, more often than not you'll be on the wrong side of the profit. That's why you want to research a company before you invest because almost nothing goes straight up without a few bumps in the road. Every time you purchase a stock, you have to look at it the same way you would if your neighbor asked you to invest in his company. Would you do it without inquiring what the company was about? How long it had been in business? Was it profitable? Or, would you act on the investment because you heard a couple of people talking around town about what a great little company he or she had? Anyway, go ahead and speculate if you choose but be aware that's what you're doing and please don't speculate with more than 5% of your wealth after you're worth at least 6 figures unless it's in your *own* enterprise!

Chapter 10

STAYING RICH!

Ahh...this is the hard part! Maybe harder than *getting* rich! There are so many temptations! There's an old saying, "Fear and greed govern the stock market." And it's not so much "fear" that you'll lose your money as it is fear that you'll "miss out" on an opportunity! Fear and greed will always try to be with you.

Once you achieve wealth, you'll find yourself between a rock and hard place. You'll go from trying to win to trying not to lose. When you're trying to win, the feeling is exhilarating! It's euphoric! But once you have it, you're trying to protect it. You go from a "winning" attitude to a "Not losing" demeanor. You realize that your wealth has you trapped. It took so much to make it you don't want to lose it!

Well, remember this: Life is risk. When you wake in the morning and get into your car you're taking a risk. Risk is always with you. Living life is a risk. A risk that you won't eat contaminated food, a risk that you won't run into a beer truck on the way to work.

A risk that people who love you may not love you anymore. There is risk everywhere, all around you! Risk is a part of everyday life. So what do you do? You avoid *unnecessary* risk!

Nobody wants to lose all they've worked so hard to gain. Nobody. Once you've attained a net worth of a million dollars or more, you need to be more discerning in where your dollars go. That doesn't mean you don't invest in 'Start ups' or high risk ventures. But it does mean that no more than 10% of your wealth goes in that direction.

Remember, once you've achieved financial security you want to stay there. Once you're there, seemingly out of nowhere individuals will arrive at your door step with "can't lose, get rich" schemes. How did they find out about your wealth? Well, that's a whole other story. Remember this: Their job is to sell you on the idea and your job is to reject it.

Ask yourself: "Do I really need more money?" There's a difference between "need" and "want"! We all want more money but if it's at the expense of your current peace of mind, it's just not worth it. Peace of mind is everything!

It's true that wealthy people live longer than the average citizen. I believe that's because wealth has a calming of the nerves. When you get there, you'll know what I mean. The wealthy can also afford the very best health care and maintenance. If you put that wealth at imprudent risk too often, you will lose your wealth and your calm.

Being broke feels bad. Being wealthy and then being broke feels worse. Because, in that case, you feel stupid. You had it and lost it. In fact, it could be argued you *have* been stupid. And believe this: All those friends and relatives who found you when you had money will somehow disappear, no matter how generous you were to them, making those "short term pay off" decisions.

Financial Advisors

His or her job is to keep you wealthy. 50% of doctors graduated in the lower half of their class. Likewise, there are good and bad financial advisors. You only need one if they have a stellar financial background and maybe not even then. Remember this too: They aren't free. So they better be worth their fees.

Chapter 11

"WHY NOT YOU?"

Recently, a Marist-McClatchy poll found that eight out of 10 Americans no longer believe they can achieve the American Dream.

Most of us were born into a middle class family or lower. Perhaps this doesn't apply to you but remember in earlier chapters we talked about the "unspoken" script as a youngster that says: *"Work real hard and study in school and one day you'll have a nice job and a comfortable income but you won't be rich because "rich" is for people above our station!"*

Well, your parents didn't write that down for you but you could sense it in their daily attitude. If you can't imagine and expect yourself to be wealthy one day, you've put a road block on yourself that you will never be able to overcome. I believe it's the single biggest reason most individuals *aren't* rich. They don't think they have a "right" to be wealthy!

And so just in case you've become a victim of this mind set, I have a little exercise for you. At first it may seem silly and frivolous but I promise you, over time it will work on you and change your mindset and your life.

Every day, at least once a day, (more if you can find the alone time) I want you to look in a mirror and say these words: *"I have a right to be rich! I plan to be rich very soon! Everyone else has a right to be rich so why not me?"*

The mirror simply intensifies the thought. If a mirror isn't handy, just repeat it to yourself as often as you can through the day. It truly becomes a self fulfilling prophecy.

The overwhelming majority of millionaires in the U.S. have a net worth of between $1 million and $10 million dollars. That is the level of wealth that *most* of us can make in one generation.

Every single human in this country with average intelligence and a treasure map guide book can attain at least a million dollars in their lifetime. There are exceptions who have made much more and others who have never made it. But those who have not made their million or more are either those who don't care to or, in most cases have made bad, short term payoff decisions along the way.

Otherwise, it's a given. *You'll get there.*

Comforting isn't it? And it's real. Follow my lead in this handbook and you'll find yourself there faster than you imagine. It's not out of your reach. In fact, the odds are very much in your favor that you will be a wealthy individual.

And don't worry about no inheritance. A little more than 80% of today's wealthy are first generation.

When you get there, you're probably going to drive a late model (but used) vehicle. You're going to own an upscale (but relatively modest) home. There's a 50/50 chance your kids will attend a private school.

In addition, you're going to be as secretive as possible about your wealth. Because if you aren't the dogs of society will get the scent of your money and attack!

"Money Screams! Wealth is Silent."

Chapter 12

(THE 10 RICHEST PEOPLE ALIVE)

Not many girls on this list but that will change soon after a couple read this hand book.
Meanwhile:

#1   Bill Gates Net Worth $79.2 Billion (Source: Microsoft founder)

#2   Carlos Slim Net Worth $77.1 Billion (Source: Telecom)

#3   Warren Buffett Net Worth $72.7 Billion (Source: Berkshire Hathaway)

#4   Amancio Ortega Net Worth $64.5 Billion (Source: Zara) `

#5   Larry Ellison Net Worth $54.3 Billion (Source: Oracle)

#6 Charles Koch Net Worth $42.9 Billion (Source: Diversified Investments)

#6 (tie) David Koch Net Worth $42.9 Billion (Source: Diversified Investments)

#8 Christy Walton Net Worth $41.7 Billion (Source: Walmart)

#9 Jim Walton Net Worth 40.6 Billion (Source: Walmart)

#10 Liliane Bettencourt Net Worth $40.1 Billion (Source: L'Oreal)

#11 YOU! (Soon!)

The Richest guy who ever lived was a fellow named **"Mansa Musa"** he was the king of Timbuktu. (That's not a joke). Musa's African kingdom was the largest producer of gold in the world at a time when gold was in very high demand. History tells tales of a pilgrimage he made to Mecca during which he spent so lavishly that it caused a currency crises in Egypt! They say his wealth was so large that no one has ever been able to describe or comprehend it. He died in 1337 at the age of 57. **Caesar Augustus** did pretty well too! At one point, he had personal wealth equivalent to one-fifth of the Roman economy which is the equivalent of about $5 trillion in 2015 dollars.

So, maybe a thousand years from now they'll be writing about how you acquired billions and lived happily ever after. I don't think you'll ever own Egypt but maybe Mexico or the Baja Peninsula if they're for sale or you're in a conquering mood. After all, Larry Ellison, the founder of Oracle (first generation billionaire) now owns the entire Hawaiian Island of Lanai! Whew! Rumors are he outbid Bill Gates.

So head on out young lady! You too young man! Go and seek your fame and fortune and carry this handbook with you. Consider it your treasure map.

www.ingramcontent.com/pod-product-compliance
Lightning Source LLC
Chambersburg PA
CBHW060048210326
41520CB00009B/1305